Successful Flexible Working in a week

**CATHY SMITH
FIONA McWILLIAMS**

Hodder & Stoughton

A MEMBER OF THE HODDER HEADLINE GROUP

Orders: please contact Bookpoint Ltd, 39 Milton Park, Abingdon, Oxon OX14 4TD. Telephone: (44) 01235 400414, Fax: (44) 01235 400454. Lines are open from 9.00 - 6.00, Monday to Saturday, with a 24 hour message answering service.
Email address: orders@bookpoint.co.uk

British Library Cataloguing in Publication Data
A catalogue record for this title is available from The British Library

ISBN 0 340 71189 2

First published 1998
Impression number   10   9   8   7   6   5   4   3   2   1
Year   2004   2003   2002   2001   2000   1999   1998

Copyright © 1998 Cathy Smith and Fiona McWilliams

All rights reserved. No part of this publication may be reproduced or transmitted in any form or by any means, electronic or mechanical, including photocopy, recording, or any information storage and retrieval system, without permission in writing from the publisher or under licence from the Copyright Licensing Agency Limited. Further details of such licences (for reprographic reproduction) may be obtained from the Copyright Licensing Agency Limited, of 90 Tottenham Court Road, London W1P 9HE.

Cover photo from Zefa Photo Library.

Typeset by Multiplex Techniques Ltd, St Mary Cray, Kent.
Printed in Great Britain for Hodder & Stoughton Educational, a division of Hodder Headline Plc, 338 Euston Road, London NW1 3BH by Cox and Wyman, Reading, Berkshire.

the Institute of Management
FOUNDATION

The Institute of Management (IM) exists to promote the development, exercise and recognition of professional management. The Institute embraces all levels of management from student to chief executive and supports its own Foundation which provides a unique portfolio of services for all managers, enabling them to develop skills and achieve management excellence.

For information on the various levels and benefits of membership, please contact:

> Department HS
> Institute of Management
> Cottingham Road
> Corby
> Northants NN17 1TT
> Tel: 01536 204222
> Fax: 01536 201651

This series is commissioned by the Institute of Management Foundation.

CONTENTS

Introduction		5
Sunday	Flexible working today	6
Monday	Flexible working hours	16
Tuesday	Numerical flexibility	29
Wednesday	The flexible workplace	42
Thursday	Family-friendly policies	55
Friday	Secondments and sabbaticals	66
Saturday	Implementing flexible working	79

INTRODUCTION

Although the traditional image of flexible working is that of low-skilled, low-paid, part-time work, it is estimated that as many as one third of UK workers are now in non-standard employment. An increasing number are found at technical and managerial levels, and while it is true that some people are forced into part-time or temporary employment in order to find work, for many, flexible working has become a matter of choice. While in some cases flexible working is imposed by employers, it is more commonly driven by employee demands.

Flexible working practices are leading to fundamental changes in the workplace and are challenging the way we think about work. They are placing new demands on today's managers and have facilitated a new type of relationship between employee and organisation. In *Successful Flexible Working in a Week*, we shall consider:

Sunday	Flexible working today
Monday	Flexible working hours
Tuesday	Numerical flexibility
Wednesday	The flexible workplace
Thursday	Family-friendly policies
Friday	Secondments and sabbaticals
Saturday	Implementing flexible working

Employers need to develop the flexibility to meet both their own business goals and their employees' needs. *Successful Flexible Working in a Week* looks at flexible working from the viewpoint of both organisations and individuals.

Flexible working today

Today's businesses, faced with global competition, are striving to cut costs and become more responsive to customers. This means that they are under greater pressure than ever before, and so are their staff. One of the results of this increased pressure is that employees are often required to work long hours on paid or unpaid overtime. Flexible working is increasingly seen as a means for organisations to achieve their business objectives while reducing the stress on employees and helping them to juggle their work and private lives.

Today, we will ask:

- What is flexible working?
- What are the trends towards flexible working?
- Who are the flexible workers?
- What are the reasons for introducing flexible working?
- How does flexible working affect management practices?
- What are the benefits and problems of flexible working?

What is flexible working?

Traditionally, individuals work between 35 and 40 hours a week, for 52 weeks a year, less annual leave and bank holidays, on a permanent contract and on an employer's premises. Flexible working practices, on the other hand, differ in terms of the hours worked, the length of contract or the place of work. They can be divided into three main categories:

1 those which give both employees and employers flexibility in the management of time. These include flexitime, annualised hours, shift work, and part-time work, as well as breaks from employment to care for dependants or to take a sabbatical;
2 those which allow employers to cater for peaks or troughs in demand through numerical flexibility, for example by the employment of temporary staff or contractors;
3 those which allow flexibility regarding the place of work, such as teleworking.

What are the trends towards flexible working?

Flexible working has grown by 30 per cent over the past 10 years to the extent that now only just over 50 per cent of the workforce holds a permanent, full-time job. Consider the following:

- A quarter of the UK workforce works part-time
- Temporary working increased by more than 40 per cent between 1992 and 1996, and the number of temporary workers now stands at around 1.5 million
- More than one third of organisations use flexible-hours contracts, and more than one quarter use job sharing
- Teleworking has seen a fivefold increase in the past five years

Who are the flexible workers?

The common view is that most flexible workers are women, holding low-skilled, poorly-paid jobs which are held in low esteem both by the employer and by the job holder. The evidence suggests, however, that this is no longer valid. Many flexible workers are men. While the growth in the number of women in part-time work was relatively flat between 1984 and 1996, the number of men in part-time work grew by 108 per cent. Furthermore, flexible workers are found at all levels in organisations. Nearly half of the companies recently surveyed by the Institute of Management said that they use flexible employees at management and professional levels, and one in four said that technical grades also had flexible workers. Although the majority of flexible workers are still found in clerical, secretarial and other support roles, flatter organisations have led to an increase in responsibilities at all levels. The importance of information and knowledge has led to the revaluing and upgrading of administrative staff who now require a broad range of skills and a high degree of technological competence to fulfil their tasks. Flexible workers undertake tasks, such as information analysis, financial management and customer care, which are central to the success of today's organisations. Today's flexible workers are as likely to be skilled data analysts as they are cooks and cleaners.

What are the reasons for introducing flexible working?

Employers and individuals have distinct reasons for using flexible working patterns. In many cases these reasons coalesce, however, to work to the advantage of both sides.

Organisational reasons
Increased competition has led to pressure to decrease costs and increase productivity. Organisations also need to respond rapidly to change and to maximise the speed to market of new products and services. Flexibility gives employers the ability to use resources more efficiently, deploying skilled staff as and when they are needed.

Changing customer demands have led to the need to improve speed of response outside the normal working day, for example, to 24-hour banking and financial services, 24-hour computer and technical support services, late-night

SUNDAY

shopping, and round-the-clock news and entertainment.

Demand for a product or service varies from a daily up to a seasonal level. Traditional working time does not allow much flexibility without incurring extra costs, such as overtime. Flexible working practices, however, match the availability of employees with demand.

Technological change (brought about by the convergence of telecommunications and computing) has allowed organisations to change their working practices. Technologies such as the Internet and video-conferencing have removed barriers of time and place. Organisations can now bring in staff who are physically located halfway across the country or halfway across the world, working in different time zones.

Social and demographic changes in the population have resulted in more older people, single parents and dual-income couples in the workforce. Organisations cannot afford to ignore such people, many of whom are only able to opt into the workplace through flexible working.

Legislative pressure. Equal-opportunities legislation has made it increasingly necessary for employers to be more flexible in their provisions for maternity leave and the return of women to work.

Pressure from employees (see below). There is a growing recognition of the benefits of a motivated, committed workforce. Employment practices which provide *all* staff with rewarding job opportunities as well as a chance of a fulfilling life outside work are not just morally desirable but also increasingly an important way of attracting and retaining skilled staff.

Individuals' reasons
Lifestyles. Increasingly, men as well as women are looking to balance their work with other aspects of their life, which may involve caring for dependants, carrying out volunteer work, following leisure pursuits, or simply finding more time to relax. This wish for a work–life balance seems to be particularly true of young people. A Coopers & Lybrand survey of final-year students in 10 countries found that they are no longer prepared to sacrifice their personal lives for their careers. They are more interested in achieving a balanced lifestyle than they are in a competitive salary. Similarly, people born between 1963 and 1981 (often referred to as Generation X) view themselves as independent and creative, and place a high emphasis on getting their work done through managing their own time and setting their own schedules. They like to base their relationship with their employer on mutual respect.

SUNDAY

Career choice. Some individuals value mobility of work because they do not want to tie themselves to one organisation for long periods of time, for reasons of temperament or because their skills are highly marketable. Others combine one job with another (perhaps unpaid).

Force of circumstance. In the wake of the restructurings of the 1980s and 1990s, some people have had no choice but to get some kind of job which may be of a more flexible nature than they would have liked.

Domestic responsibilities. There are more women in the workforce than ever before, but women are still the primary carers. They are often in favour of flexible working because they may have young children or elderly relatives to look after. Cases of a few high-profile women who have given up highly-paid jobs to care for their family have highlighted the need for more flexible work patterns to enable people to cope with their work and home responsibilities.

S U N D A Y

How does flexible working affect management practices?

Flexible working involves a greater investment of management time, effort and commitment than traditional forms of working. This can be seen in all phases, but is particularly true at the start. Flexible working, like any other management initiative, involves change: the effective management of change therefore becomes an important factor. Overcoming entrenched attitudes, as well as feelings of insecurity and uncertainty which change brings, is always a difficult task. Taking time to reach agreement on change is the only way in which resistance can be overcome and new ways of working can be successfully introduced.

As the number of flexible workers increases, so organisations have to compete for the best, and most skilled, flexible workers. Companies should offer similar benefits to full-time and flexible staff, including training and development. There is a need to implement career and personal planning for all staff and to help all employees develop their skills beyond the immediate needs of current tasks. These skills should be transferable and not directly connected to any one job.

Because some flexible workers, such as teleworkers, will be working out of sight of their manager and co-workers for the majority of the time, the issue of trust becomes more important. Managers therefore need to significantly enhance their skills in communication and team-building in order to ensure the effective integration of flexible employees. They should also recognise that time spent at the office does not equate to productivity.

SUNDAY

What are the benefits and problems of flexible working?

Well-managed flexible working practices can lead to an improved corporate reputation for being a caring, modern employer, and to a widening of the skills pool. The main benefit, however, is increased productivity and improved customer service, which is achieved through:

- increased job satisfaction
- improved morale
- increased commitment and loyalty to the organisation
- lower absence rates
- better use of time as flexible workers are often more disciplined in their time management
- lower stress levels as family and work commitments become easier to balance

SUNDAY

On the other hand, flexible working can result in declining morale and lower employee commitment if it smacks of downsizing, unpredictable or insecure employment, attempts to force employees into patterns of work which are unsuitable for them, low pay and few opportunities for training and promotion. Some uses of flexible working can be seen as part of an uncaring and irresponsible attitude on the part of employers. It can also lead to the danger of developing a two-tier workforce of haves and have nots.

It is essential to establish a fair deal which balances employer and employee benefits. Introducing flexible working practices means that organisations are asking people to change their way of life. In addition to the advantages for the organisation, managers must look at changes from the point of view of the individuals who will be affected, and find an arrangement that will suit all parties.

Summary

Today, we have looked at the trend towards flexible working and at the benefits and problems which this brings. Tomorrow we begin to look at the range of flexible working practices available by considering flexible working hours.

MONDAY

Flexible working hours

Flexibility in hours of work means that organisations can extend their opening hours or production capability, and cater for variations in demand without working excessive overtime. Individuals too find flexible working hours a helpful employment option in reconciling the (sometimes) conflicting demands of work and personal life.

Today we will examine the wide range of alternative options to the traditional 9–5 working day. We will consider:

- shiftwork
- annualised hours
- zero hours
- ad hoc working
- flexitime
- call-in well days
- part-time working
- job share
- term-time working
- phased retirement

Shiftwork

Shiftworking is one of the longest-established forms of flexible working, and offers employers the ability to maintain production or to provide a service beyond the normal working day or week. While some companies have 24-hour shift coverage seven days a week, others may only need to cover production for shorter periods, for example

MONDAY

18 hours a day, Monday to Friday. Shiftworking used to be the preserve of manual workers – only those managers directly involved with production needed to work shifts. The growth in the use of new technologies and the increasing requirement for operating across time zones, however, means that more professionals are moving to shiftwork.

Shiftworking is not always popular with employees as it is seen to affect their body rhythms, family and social lives, and its introduction (or a change to an existing shift pattern) is often cited as a cause of industrial action.

Annualised hours

In an annualised-hours system, working hours are averaged across a year and employees are then contracted to work a given number of hours per year, rather than the more traditional number of hours per week. Hours are worked when demand is present, and the need for paid overtime is consequently greatly diminished.

Earnings are determined on a similar basis, but a fixed weekly or monthly salary is paid regardless of the hours worked. Although some employees fear annual hours will diminish their level of earnings by reducing overtime, many employers consolidate an amount equivalent to typical overtime payments into an annual salary.

Some concern has been expressed about the impact that the European Working Time Directive (which restricts the number of hours an individual can work) may have on annualised-hours schemes. Because this Directive allows hours worked to be averaged over a four-month period, however, it is unlikely to have too adverse an effect.

Annualised hours can apply to the whole workforce, but most usually cover manual shiftworkers.

Case study – annual hours

Dutton Engineering is a sheet metal working company with an order book which is unpredictable. In order to eliminate wasted time and to match employee hours with customer requirements, Dutton introduced an annual-hours system. This was part of a wider restructuring package which included the removal of premium payments for overtime, a new payment system, revised grading structures and changes in working practices to develop a team culture.

The basic requirement is to work 1,770 hours a year with a reserve of a further 160 hours which are intended for sickness, medical or dental appointments, rework and peak production. Working hours are arranged according to customer demand, and during slack

> periods a short week is worked, and during busy periods a long week. Employees are now salaried and enjoy greater predictability of earnings through equal instalments of pay. Payment for the reserve hours is included in the basic salary regardless of whether or not the company calls on these hours. There is also a 20-per-cent profit-related bonus paid monthly.
>
> Annual hours have meant that time at work is spent more effectively. There is no longer an incentive to stretch work to fit the day, but rather to finish the work and go home. Rework takes place during the reserved hours, so there is a positive incentive to get things right first time. On the other hand, team members sometimes have to work into the night, but this is a trade-off and is understood and accepted. Urgent orders which arrive after the workforce have gone home are fulfilled by means of a bleeper system. Each team has a bleeper holder who, when alerted, brings together a team with the necessary skills to manufacture the item requested.
>
> Source: *How to Transform Your Company and Enjoy It!*, Ken Lewis and Stephen Lytton, Management Books 2000, 1997.

Zero hours

Zero-hours working is an arrangement under which employees are on-call and available to work at the convenience of their employer, but with no guarantee of any work. Payment is made not for the time spent on-call but only for any hours actually worked. Zero-hours arrangements are most frequently encountered in the service sector and encompass a range of occupations from nursing, teaching and banking to catering and retailing. They provide employers with the capability of managing work fluctuations without incurring additional costs.

MONDAY

Zero-hours workers are commonly perceived to have few (if any) contractual rights, and some employers have exploited this position to exclude them from maternity, redundancy or sick pay. However, recent case law has demonstrated that zero-hours workers do have employment rights, and this is gradually impacting on employment practices.

Ad hoc working

Ad hoc working arrangements share some of the features offered by zero-hours contracts, particularly the non-guarantee of work. There are several differences between the two types of work, however:

- Ad hoc employees do not have a contract of employment
- There is no obligation on an ad hoc worker to take up an offer of work
- Ad hoc arrangements tend to be between an individual and several organisations (or one organisation with a range of outlets)

MONDAY

Supply teaching (which gives schools the flexibility to call on an extra teacher only when they need one) is probably the best known and most widely practised form of ad hoc working.

> ### Case study – supply teaching
>
> After the birth of my first son, I did not want to return to teaching full-time, but was drawn to the idea of supply teaching where I could largely dictate my hours of work. Although I was initially rather nervous of this new challenge which exposes you to a variety of schools and age groups, I soon adapted and found that it suited me very well. I have continued supply teaching off and on for the last seven years.
>
> The flexibility offered by this kind of work has allowed me to decide when and how I want to work without the commitment of the extra workload I would experience in a contracted teaching post (even a part-time one). It has also enabled me to have long stretches of time off to have two more children and to travel abroad with my husband. As I hope to return to permanent work one day, supply teaching has meant that I can keep my skills up to date and maintain my confidence. The one big disadvantage I have found (and one which prevents many people from following a similar path) is the difficulty of finding child care when hours are so erratic.

Flexitime

Flexitime is a system which allows employees to arrange their working hours (within prescribed limits). It was introduced to the UK during the 1970s – originally as a method of reducing traffic congestion by removing the 'rush hour'. Today, it is one of the best known methods of flexible working, although it is mostly confined to office-based staff.

MONDAY

Flexitime systems are based on a set number of hours to be worked each week, with 'core' periods (typically 10.00am–12 noon and 2.00pm–4.00pm) when employees must be at work. Around this core (and providing business needs are met) employees are able to determine their hours of work. Most schemes allow employees to carry over either a debit or credit of hours between weeks or months, and normally allow a day of 'flexileave' each month.

Employers often find that a flexitime system results in reductions in absenteeism and overtime, can aid in recruitment, and helps to manage variations in workflow effectively.

Case study – flexitime

I am a tax inspector with the Inland Revenue where a new flexitime system has recently been introduced, along with a new office structure which brings together more people in bigger offices.

We still work 37 hours a week. Previously we had to work the core hours of 10–11.30am and 2.30–4.00pm, but now we can work any time between 7.00am and 6.45pm as long as we let our colleagues know our plans. We can carry forward 18.5 hours, credit or debit, into the next four-week period, and twice a year we can take a whole week off based on accumulated flexitime. Some offices, however, now insist that visits to the doctor and dentist be taken in our own time.

The advantage to us is that we can better balance our personal and working lives. The advantage to customers is that the Revenue has been able to extend the opening hours of its enquiry points. The Revenue wants to further increase the number of opening hours, however. At the start there will be enough volunteers to cover these hours, but some of us (and the unions) are worried that when the

MONDAY

volunteers leave, other employees will be forced to work these unsocial hours.

On the whole, though, the system is an improvement for both employees and customers. It has only been made possible by the introduction of bigger offices where there are large numbers of people to cover for each other. Even with such a radical system (with no core time), there are still more people in the office at any one time than there were before.

Call-in well days

Call-in well days are a recent development which acknowledges the fact that some employees sometimes call-in sick when they need a day off. By allowing employees to take up to two days per year as call-in well days, organisations recognise that personal needs occasionally must take priority, and are able to develop a more honest relationship with employees.

MONDAY

Part-time working

In the past, part-time workers tended to be found in poorly-paid, low-skilled jobs, and were often disregarded as not being fully committed to their employer. This situation is beginning to improve. Almost any type of position can be filled on a part-time basis nowadays, including management and other highly skilled positions. Moreover, part-timers now enjoy equal protection with full-time colleagues under the employment laws, although many still experience lower rates of pay, reduced pension rights and limited sick-pay entitlement.

A growing proportion of the workforce works part-time. This increase is due to a number of reasons, but is principally because:

- employers need to recruit extra staff to meet demand as banks and shops begin to open at times more convenient to the public. Frequently, part-time employees are seen as a solution.
- employees are beginning to demand of their employers that part-time working arrangements be made available to them. This is particularly true of mothers returning to work who feel unable to undertake a full-time job.

Case study – part-time working

I began working part-time after I returned from maternity leave. Although my department has a high proportion of women, I was the first to return after maternity leave, and although I wanted to go back, I was concerned about balancing work and home responsibilities. In the end, I plucked up the courage to ask my manager if he would consider allowing me to come back part-time –

MONDAY

> to which he very bravely agreed. My contract was changed to allow me to work for three and a half days for one year and then return to full-time employment. The arrangement has worked very well from both my point of view and that of my manager. I really enjoy the extra day and a half with my son and believe that it helps me not to feel guilty whilst I'm at work. I think my manager recognises that a part-time employee gives him extra flexibility in his staffing arrangements. Since beginning to work part-time, I have started to 'hot-desk' – moving to whichever desk in the department is vacant at any time – which has freed up physical resources. I now take on routine tasks from anyone who is working on an additional project or is on leave. The arrangement must be working as my contract has just been amended to allow permanent part-time working.

Job share

Job sharing involves two people carrying out the duties and responsibilities of one full-time post. Working time, salary and benefits are divided between them. Job sharing is suitable for any level of employee, but in practice few senior positions are occupied by job sharers. To operate successfully, job sharers need to be able to communicate well and to maintain an excellent working relationship between each other.

Job sharing has many benefits to offer organisations:

- **The experience, knowledge and personal qualities of two individuals are available together in one post.**
- **Job sharers typically demonstrate a high level of commitment both to their employer and to ensuring the success of the job share.**

- A job-share arrangement means continuity of cover for a key position at times of holiday or sick leave, with one half of the share covering for the other. There have even been cases of one half of a share covering the maternity leave of the other.

Some line managers are, however, reluctant to employ job sharers as they expect an increased administrative workload. Although job sharing is not widespread, many organisations impose a limit on the number of job shares available in each department, fearing that too many in one place will cause an administrative nightmare.

Term-time working

Term-time working allows employees to work during school terms only, and so is ideal for those with responsibilities for children. Annual leave and salary are assigned on a pro-rata basis (although salary is frequently paid in monthly instalments across the full year). Term-time working arrangements are limited beyond their natural (educational) sector, however, as holiday times are often very busy and other employees will want to take leave at this time as well. Other sectors which offer term-time contracts include retailing and catering where staff working under such arrangements can be replaced by students on vacation.

Phased retirement

Recruitment problems caused by an ageing population, and employees' worries about a reduced income during retirement, have led to an increase in the practice of phased retirement (also known as gradual, partial or part-time retirement). This form of winding-down allows employees to retire over a period of time (anywhere between six months and five years).

Phased retirement allows an organisation to retain the skills and experience of older employees for longer while a period of transition from one member of staff to another takes place. This can be important in senior positions where the training of a replacement and the building of trust may take time. Phased retirement also allows employees to adjust gradually to the changes that retirement brings. UK tax laws, however, prevent people from drawing a pension and receiving a salary from the same employer. Until this problem is addressed, phased retirement is unlikely to gain in popularity.

MONDAY

Summary

Today we have looked at a variety of flexible-working-hours arrangements and their pros and cons for both employer and employee. Tomorrow we will consider temporary working and outsourcing which allow organisations flexibility in the numbers of people they employ.

TUESDAY

Numerical flexibility

In *The Age of Unreason*, Charles Handy forecast that by the year 2000 half of all paid workers would be temporary or part-time. He suggested that organisations would consist of a core of better-qualified workers supplemented by outside contractors whose services were bought when required. This forecast has been supported by research carried out by the Institute of Management and Manpower which has found that 89 per cent of the organisations surveyed use temporary and part-time workers and 70 per cent outsource some services.

Given the highly competitive nature of today's markets, some employers require flexible employment strategies which allow them to meet peaks and troughs in demand easily and quickly, or to concentrate on their core business (what they are best at) and contract out peripheral activities to others. Although such policies can have an adverse and unsettling effect on some individual workers, others are finding that numerical flexibility can benefit them by allowing them to build diversity and variety into their careers.

Today we will look at some of the ways of achieving numerical flexibility and focus on the associated benefits. We shall consider:

- why temporary work is increasing
- short-term and fixed-term contracts
- interim managers and independent consultants
- contractors and subcontractors
- portfolio working
- outsourcing

TUESDAY

Why temporary work is increasing

Research carried out by the Institute for Employment Studies suggests that although temporary workers only make up 9 per cent of the workforce, over 50 per cent of employers use them at one time or another. Temporary workers are employed for a variety of reasons:

- to cover short-term absences (such as maternity or sick leave and holidays)
- to determine (on a trial basis) if the individual is suitable for permanent employment, or whether the job they are carrying out needs to be done on a permanent basis
- to bring in specialist skills, which may be needed to carry out 'one-off' projects
- to match seasonal variations in the work required

Traditionally, 'temping' has been the preserve of those such as secretaries, packers or assembly-line workers – in other words, those jobs classed as skilled or semi-skilled rather than professional. Because of the demographic and organisational changes we discussed on Sunday, this picture is now changing. Managers and other professional staff are recognising the opportunities that temporary employment offers, and some are opting for this in preference to traditional, full-time or permanent employment.

This group consists mostly of:

- those who are unable to commit to permanent/full-time work (typically those with caring responsibilities)
- those who have been unemployed and see temporary work as a means back into full-time employment
- those who want a variety of challenges

- those who may not want to commit themselves to one employer for a long period
- the self-employed and those whose trades are very seldom in demand from one source all the time (such as decorators or plumbers)
- those professionals (such as software programmers, writers, designers or consultants) whose skills can be in high demand, and who see temporary work as a way to leverage the greatest payment for their efforts

Short-term and fixed-term contracts

Short- or fixed-term contracts are often used by employers as a way of staffing a project which is finite, and keeping costs to a manageable level as such contracts usually mean that redundancy payments do not need to be made when the project finishes. They inevitably, however, lead to a conflict of interest, because a short-term employee will be looking for their next job, and may even leave, before the contract comes to an end.

TUESDAY

Interim managers and independent consultants

At first sight, interim managers and independent consultants may appear to be the same animal, as both are employed on a short-term basis in order to achieve a specific objective. There are, however, significant differences between them. Interim managers share in confidential decision-making and take on line-management responsibilities in order to get 'the job' done. Independent consultants, on the other hand, gather and process information to enable them to give advice on possible solutions to problems and on how to implement these solutions. It is said that consultants recommend action, but interim managers make it happen.

Interim managers
Interim managers may be described as freelance executives commissioned for short-term assignments. They are usually required to assume immediate, high-level responsibility at short notice, and offer specialist skills and experience which may not otherwise be available in-house. Typically, interim managers are senior executives, with board-level (or near-board-level) experience, who can cope with mobility, flexibility and the uncertainty of not knowing where or what the next assignment will be.

Interim managers are normally appointed as a cost-effective way to fill unexpected vacancies or manage short-term projects such as company rescue, company relocation, a new product launch or systems installation.

TUESDAY

Interim managers can bring organisations many advantages over the permanent employment of an individual. They offer:

- accumulated experience
- strong leadership skills
- short-notice availability
- distance from company politics and an objective view of situations and processes
- a lack of interest in protecting their career progress
- a lack of threat to other staff as they are only employed on short-term contracts

Before employing interim managers, organisations should take steps to ensure that they get the best value for money because it is not a cheap option. These include a need to:

- ensure that the interim manager 'fits in' with the culture of the organisation
- be prepared for things to happen quickly – the experience an interim manager can offer usually means that they need only a very short time to get things moving
- set clear objectives

TUESDAY

> ## Case study: call in an interim manager
>
> It was a situation that many large companies face. The Group Board decided to divest itself of a company not deemed part of the core business. With existing resources pushed to the limit, and the loss of a key staff member, the Board decided to appoint an *interim manager* to handle the transaction.
>
> Assuming the Managing Director's position, the interim manager was charged with the responsibility of keeping the business ticking over with the objective of achieving a fast, effective sale. Staff morale was low, as many people feared for their jobs, and clients were uneasy over the prospect of new ownership. Building up and retaining the motivation of staff whilst allaying the fears of clients became a key part of keeping the business moving as negotiations were taking place.
>
> The transaction took four months to complete: a successful sale enhancing the reputation of the business, a greatly satisfied parent company, and not a single job lost.
>
> For the company, interim management means hiring expertise that may not be available within its hierarchy, or that cannot be spared at the time. The interim manager can be in position within one to two weeks, is sensibly over-qualified for the job and having completed the assignment leaves the company. No fuss sorting out pension plans, benefits or National Insurance, and no expenditure on unnecessary resources.
>
> *Source:* Ashton Penney Partnership Limited, Tel: 0171 580 8490.

Independent consultants

Independent consultants tend to specialise in one or two areas (such as project management, training or business appraisal). Like interim managers, they typically have many years' experience of their chosen discipline and enjoy helping organisations work through problems or opportunities.

Independent consultants are often brought in by organisations to offer:

- *expertise* – by specialising in one or two areas, consultants can provide 'state of the art' advice.
- *an independent viewpoint* – a consultant can bring fresh vision to a problem, seeing those things which are unclear to those on the inside, or saying those things which permanent employees are afraid of saying. By being seen to obtain impartial advice, an organisation may find staff more willing to participate in a programme of change.

Checklist for successful management consultancy projects
The services of independent consultants can often prove to be a valuable investment providing certain rules are followed. Organisations must:

1 allow enough time for the whole assignment;
2 define the area of the assignment rigorously;
3 establish what they want the consultant to do;
4 identify the necessary steps involved in the task;
5 select the consultant with care;
6 explain to employees why the consultant is being employed;
7 measure the progress towards a solution.

TUESDAY

> ## Case study – independent consultant
>
> I've been an independent consultant for over 10 years. Previously I'd worked in a variety of human-resource functions for a number of companies in the chemical/pharmaceutical sector. Although I enjoyed my work, I found the petty politics very wearing, and having had to break the news to two of my close colleagues that they were being made redundant was the final straw. I decided enough was enough, and having drawn up a business plan and consulted colleagues who had taken a similar route previously, I handed in my notice and began to work for myself.
>
> Initially, my former employer gave me a two-year contract to continue to run their training programmes on the basis of five days work per month. This provided me with some security whilst I established myself and began working with other organisations. Although training still forms a significant chunk of my contracts, it is now supplemented by other areas of work. Some of my projects have included individual career counselling, helping boards of directors to operate as a team, and designing and introducing an appraisal scheme.
>
> Although there are many pressures to being independent – continuing to carry out paid work whilst looking for the next paid contract is just one of the bugbears – the compensations (no 'in-fighting', the satisfaction of knowing you've really made a difference) far outweigh these. If I were to be offered a permanent post, I know I wouldn't accept it.

Contractors and subcontractors

A contractor is someone who works for an organisation but is not an employee of that organisation. Although this definition includes those who fall into the category of interim manager or independent consultant, a contractor is an individual with key technical skills (such as civil engineering or software programming). Contractors often bring in subcontractors – people whom they do not employ but who have the relevant skills and expertise to ensure that the job the contractor is working on is completed. Subcontractors are therefore employed one step away from the organisation.

Portfolio working

With part-time and temporary jobs becoming more common at all levels of organisations, and with a greater need to maintain some control over the division between working and personal life, some individuals choose to combine two or more jobs in a 'portfolio' career – a term first coined by Charles Handy. These jobs may be linked (two computing positions, for example) or may be quite distinct (for example, a teacher for three days a week and a gardener or carer the rest of the time). Most jobs in a portfolio career are not permanent positions, so the

TUESDAY

portfolio changes over time – and as portfolio workers characteristically enjoy challenges, this is often seen as a benefit rather than a pitfall.

> ## Case study – portfolio working
>
> I work with computers and changed from full-time to part-time employment about 10 years ago. Much more recently I've moved away from working for one employer to working with a number of different groups. Currently, I'm developing a database for a charity (working mainly at home), with occasional on-site computer support visits to two education groups based in a nearby town. Because I work from home for part of the time, I've also been able to fulfil a life-long ambition by becoming a reserve fireman.
>
> I've gained huge benefits from this way of working – I can be quite demanding of employers, and being able to divide my time between different ones stops me becoming too frustrated with them. I've been lucky enough to be able to be selective in the organisations I've worked with, which means I can work with people I like without the drudgery of a 9-to-5 slog day after day. I enjoy the fact that there are always new challenges, and working part-time gives me time for interests in life other than work – involvement with a charity, music, motorcycling and raising my daughter. Of course, there are disadvantages to working as I do. It's difficult to get a sense of continuity, and I do miss the daily interactions of seeing the same people every day. It can also be difficult to earn enough to make it financially worthwhile – I don't want to get into charging silly money as I prefer to work with charities and educational establishments. There's no security at all of course, and it can be difficult to plan even six months ahead.
>
> The reactions I've had from my peers have been interesting – some people admire the way I work whilst others think I'm crazy not to work like mad and make a packet. It still surprises me how few

> people work part-time – I don't know any other men who do! To people who are considering working in the way I do, I'd say 'Go for it' – but keep the mortgage small!

Outsourcing

Outsourcing is defined as the transfer of an organisation's internal activities to a third party under a contract which defines standards, costs and conditions expected under such an arrangement. Areas such as catering have been outsourced for several decades, but in the 1990s there has been a shift towards outsourcing integral activities, such as IT, as well. Typically, organisations choose to outsource activities because this option offers:

- the ability to focus on core activities
- a source of expertise for non-core activities
- operational, staffing and financial flexibility
- cost and efficiency savings

Organisations view outsourcing as an opportunity. Employees, on the other hand, often view outsourcing as a threat – jobs 'disappear', or they may find themselves transferred to a different organisation selected to run the activity. A careful balance needs to be struck to ensure that all parties are satisfied and understand the reasons for outsourcing.

Good interpersonal skills are required in order to help all employees manage the transition between organisations. Partnerships will need to be built with suppliers so that both parties are aware of any potential difficulties with the contract and how these might be overcome. Managers therefore need specialist skills in:

TUESDAY

- contract management
- negotiation with third parties
- balancing services coming from different sources against each other to achieve a 'whole'

Checklist for successful outsourcing

> 1 *Establish at the outset that you will only outsource the doing of an activity* – not the responsibility for the activity.
> 2 *Determine which of your organisation's processes are considered 'core' activities.* Assess the business advantages to be gained from concentrating on core activities and outsourcing the peripherals.
> 3 *Never outsource strategic, customer or financial management.*
> 4 *Attend to the anxieties and uncertainties of employees* – through clear communication of the process at all stages.
> 5 *Benchmark yourself against your competitors and partners* – to establish which activities they are outsourcing and the level of success they are experiencing.
> 6 *Select an outsourcing partner with caution* – they will be much closer to your organisation than typical suppliers and so will need to demonstrate they can share organisational values and objectives, and handle confidential information.
> 7 *Pilot the outsourcing project* – to ensure that contractual arrangements are workable and whether any adjustments are needed. Examine the consequences of the partnership breaking down.

TUESDAY

Summary

Today we have considered various ways in which organisations can achieve flexibility regarding numbers of employees. We have also examined the reasons why individuals may choose to pursue a career which consists of a variety of short-term positions. Tomorrow we will look at how flexibility in the place of work is helping organisations become more efficient.

WEDNESDAY

The flexible workplace

Today we examine how the workplace is becoming more mobile and flexible, focusing on innovations in the use of office space. These changes are being brought about by the need for organisations to speed up response times and cut costs, and by the use of telecommunications which allow people to do more of their work remotely. Such innovations are also being used more widely in response to demands made by employees who relish the flexibility, independence and enhanced efficiency of being away from the office. We shall consider:

- teleworking
- telecentres
- mobile working
- hot-desking
- hotelling
- virtual teams
- the benefits and problems of the flexible workplace

Teleworking

Teleworking involves carrying out work at a location remote from the workplace (usually, but not necessarily, at home), and communicating with the employer through the use of computer and telecommunications equipment. Such equipment allows the worker to connect to common organisational databases and groupware and to correspond with their colleagues via e-mail. It can also enable communications traffic in the reverse direction by

WEDNESDAY

allowing home-based staff to share in the handling of customer-service calls which are routed to them by an automatic call distributor, the caller unaware that they are talking to an agent working in their own home rather than in a central office.

There is evidence to show that organisations are becoming increasingly interested in various forms of teleworking and that employees too are more ready to embrace homeworking as the importance of 'owning' physical space in the office decreases and improvements in technology mean that remote workers are less isolated than in the past. A recent study by Pagoda Associates of 100 leading UK organisations predicts that one in ten white-collar staff will be working away from the office by the end of the century, rising to more than half by 2010.

WEDNESDAY

Case study – enforced remote working

I am an editorial director for a major British publishing company and commute daily from Kent to London. After an unexpected bout in hospital, I was unable to commute for several weeks and was forced to work from home.

Connectivity was the key. Armed with a home PC with full Internet access, I was able to undertake almost all the functions of my job with little negative impact. E-mail and faxes – to work colleagues, authors and advisers – meant that my study in Kent was to all intents and purposes the same place as my office in central London.

Freed from the straitjacket of commuting (and the time and energy that it consumes), my productivity was, for the most part, greater than it would have been had I been at my office. I was able to organise my work more ruthlessly than is often allowed by the inevitable interruptions and distractions in the workplace.

There were a few problems, however. Where information was not digital (incoming post to the office, for example), there were inevitable delays while it was forwarded on, and there were certain things that could only be done in the office, which placed extra burdens on close colleagues.

On the whole, though, from both my own and my company's perspective, working from home has been effective in a way it couldn't have been before the Internet. As the world becomes inexorably more digital, so this way of working becomes easier.

Although some companies employ people who work at home permanently, successful schemes show that a mix of teleworking and time at the office for briefing and social interaction is a more practical combination. Such an arrangement also makes it easier for managers to monitor and motivate employees whom they no longer see face-to-face every day.

At the moment, there is a tendency to appraise teleworkers by measuring their level of output. As teleworking spreads, however, to a wider range of jobs and workers, managers must move away from measuring quantity to take a more strategic view of productivity and develop ways of assessing quality, determining success by the question: is this contributing towards better customer service?

Checklist for introducing teleworking

1 *Carry out a feasibility study.* Include a cost–benefit analysis in the study, taking into account productivity, communication and training costs, administrative support requirements and office space.
2 *Decide which individual jobs are suitable for teleworking.*
3 *Ensure teleworkers have the necessary personal qualities and skills.* These include maturity, trustworthiness, self-sufficiency, self-discipline, good time management, communications skills and knowledge of how to use the hardware and software provided. Training and retraining may be needed – do not underestimate their importance.
4 *Put the right communications structures in place.* People must have the right tools to do the job required. Hardware and software should be compatible with the equipment used elsewhere in the organisation, have the same maintenance and insurance cover, be ergonomically sound and be kept up-to-date.

WEDNESDAY

5 *Draw up a contract.* Additional clauses to a standard employment contract should cover security of both company information and equipment, health and safety, working hours, and reporting procedures.
6 *Provide facilities for teleworkers on office days.* (See the section on hot-desking later today on pages 49–51.)
7 *Set up support systems for teleworkers.* Try to create a sense of belonging. Ensure that teleworkers receive the same newsletters, offers of training and details of social events as other employees.

(Take a look at Saturday for more general information on implementation.)

WEDNESDAY

Case study – The Virtual Office

The Virtual Office is a company that provides a service which enables other companies to work flexibly by operating wherever they choose but always to be contactable on one central telephone number. This service also makes it possible to have a central London presence without the expense of a permanent office. The Virtual Office has decided to adopt the concept of the flexible workplace for its own use. It was agreed that everyone would work from home, except the support people who were needed full-time in the office to staff the switchboard, coordinate diaries, allocate desk space and book meeting rooms for staff and clients who visited the office.

All staff have their own direct telephone numbers. These are not related to a particular extension but are routed through the switchboard to wherever that person is working, whether in the office or elsewhere. If the calls cannot be put through they are forwarded to a voice mail system where messages can be accessed and responded to at any time, or forwarded to other members of the team to be actioned or for the information to be shared.

The glue that holds the team together is e-mail. We insist that everyone copies a synopsis of all important meetings to the relevant team members. That way everyone always knows what is going on. Files are shared by sending them out as e-mail attachments; if they need to be printed out they are dealt with by the coordinator based in the office.

Members of the team usually spend about 2–3 days in the office each week. This is mainly driven by meetings with visitors. Formal meetings for the entire team are organised once a month. In between times long telephone calls supplement e-mail where exchanges can be too brief to set business problems in perspective.

WEDNESDAY

> The beauty of the flexible workplace is that people can get on with doing work at home where productivity is much higher and use their time in the office for both formal and informal meetings which also become more productive. It has brought unexpected benefits in that people with family commitments can work for us part-time. Above all, the cost of growing the business is almost nothing. A new person only costs their salary; there are no associated office costs as no-one except the office-based staff have their own desk. The biggest problem is to find somewhere to sit in the office when we are all there. Sometimes we have to go out to a local spaghetti restaurant to meet over lunch.
>
> *Source:* Richard Nissen, The Virtual Office, Tel: 0171 917 2917.

Telecentres

It is expensive to equip large numbers of homes with all the equipment which an employee might need and which is common in most offices. Furthermore, not all homes can provide the space and peace necessary for work, and some people prefer to maintain a dividing line between home and work. In such situations, telecentres or telecottages can be the answer. These centres offer shared multimedia facilities, and are either owned by one organisation providing their employees with a local work environment, or independent and used either by freelancers or by a range of employers.

Mobile working

Mobile or nomadic workers (sales people, consultants or service technicians) need tools to access the same information as that available to desk-bound workers. This

WEDNESDAY

means an interchangeable use of mobile telephony, fax and e-mail for communicating, and remote access to groupware, databases and intranets to facilitate efficient sharing and transfer of information. These tools enable mobile workers to operate efficiently at home, in an office, on the road, or in an hotel. As with home-based teleworkers, it is not just a question of supplying employees with hardware and software: the costs of training, maintenance of equipment and communications line charges, for example, must also be built in.

Mobile working can bring tangible benefits, such as improved productivity and better customer service. For example, sales people who win orders can process these themselves, on the spot (providing they are empowered to negotiate and close deals), rather than having to return to head office and wait for a clerk to handle them.

Hot-desking

Most conventional offices are only full for a fraction of the time they are open because of sickness or holidays, or because some members of staff spend a significant part of their time on customers' premises. Since this arrangement means a waste of space and other resources, some organisations are turning to hot-desking. This is defined as the removal of permanent, individual desks for some or all employees. Instead, staff are allocated a workstation when they arrive at the office, and from there they can access their own e-mail and computer network files. In this system, personal space is restricted to drawers in filing cabinets or the use of a locker, but general space is made

WEDNESDAY

available for group or team activities. Usually, those who work full-time at base are given their own desks, but in some companies *all* employees may be subject to the arrangement.

Such changes need a cautious approach, however, as the loss of personal territory can upset some employees. One answer is to provide an airport-style 'club' lounge where people can meet, collect mail, and take part in leisure and social activities.

Checklist for introducing hot-desking

> 1 *Assess the patterns of office use.* Evaluate all working processes and activities, functional requirements and demands, and social and interactive needs, as well as occupancy patterns.
> 2 *Conduct staff attitude surveys.* Gather opinions on the importance of the various forms of workspace currently offered.

3 *Reduce the number of workstations* to that consistent with the usual maximum number of people in the office at any one time.
4 *Cater for different needs*, by providing:
   - areas for quiet concentration
   - group areas for meetings, training and team collaboration
   - busy areas for telephoning
   - extensively fitted workstations for a full mix of work
   - drop-in areas with small worktop spaces
   - resident space
5 *Devise a booking system*. This should allow staff to:
   - check availability
   - reserve space
   - modify reservations
   - confirm or cancel
6 *Ensure that itinerants have a portable telephone extension* so that their calls are routed to them at whichever desk they are sitting.
7 *Provide storage space*, such as lockers or filing cabinets.
8 *Consider the psychological issues*. Some employees may regret the loss of their own office desk and space, because it leaves them feeling insecure and disenfranchised.
9 *Monitor the efficiency and effectiveness of the hot-desking facilities*. An analysis of management information supplied by the booking system can help anticipate any changes needed.

WEDNESDAY

Hotelling

Hotelling extends the concept of hot-desking. Some employees, such as sales people and consultants, spend most of their time with customers, rather than at their employer's premises. They therefore rely on their clients to provide a desk, and stay in contact with colleagues through telecommunications and computer links. When they need to work at base, they are allocated a desk on the hot-desk principle described above.

Virtual teams

Virtual teamworking allows employees to collaborate from a variety of locations, using e-mail, groupware, intranets, and video-conferencing. These staff may be teleworkers, mobile workers or people working at opposite ends of the building or on different sites. There is no longer any need for members of a team to be physically located together, although the provision of office facilities described above under 'hot-desking' is important in allowing face-to-face meetings to take place.

Technology also facilitates teamworking across organisations formally or informally. Informal external networking may benefit the organisation in some circumstances but can lead to worries about control of employees and ownership of data.

WEDNESDAY

The benefits and problems of the flexible workplace

The benefits
- Work needing concentration can be done in isolation, and time at the office can be used for human interaction
- There is an increase in productivity, typically quoted at between 30 per cent and 50 per cent
- Workers save on commuting time and costs, with knock-on environmental benefits
- Workers enjoy greater flexibility
- There is reduced stress and absenteeism, and employees become more energetic and self-motivated
- Employers incur lower office costs as savings of 25–30 per cent can be made on office space
- Teamworking is facilitated between people in different locations
- Employees are able to spend more time with customers
- People unable to take up or to continue normal office employment, in standard office hours, can be recruited or retained
- Labour markets in a wider geographic area can be tapped

The problems
- Management may fear difficulties in controlling an 'invisible' workforce
- Unless lines of communication are clear, there is a problem in ensuring that remote staff understand corporate goals and retain a sense of loyalty, and it is difficult to maintain a sense of cohesion
- Managers may resent the loss of their own space with its accompanying status

WEDNESDAY

- Remote working can lead to a feeling of social isolation; many employees therefore prefer to work in a traditional office as it represents a social milieu as well as a workplace
- There is a danger, particularly for young people entering work, that social skills will not be developed sufficiently
- The flexible workplace cannot be implemented overnight because all concerned must have a familiarity with the enabling technologies, and therefore time must be put aside for familiarisation, practice and continuing training

Summary

Today we have looked at innovative ways of working which are made possible by modern computing and telecommunications technology. One concern, which employers have about teleworking in particular, is that employees may view homeworking as a solution to child-care problems. Tomorrow we consider various ways in which organisations can help employees to find appropriate and adequate care for their children and elderly relatives.

T H U R S D A Y

Family-friendly policies

Greater numbers of women than ever before are entering the workplace – and women still carry much of the burden of caring for dependants. With the reduction in the availability of state-provided care for the elderly, sick and disabled, the caring responsibilities of those in work will continue to increase. It has been estimated that approximately one in three employees will have some form of caring responsibility at some point in their working lives.

Along with the flexible working practices discussed on Monday, a range of options exist which organisations can use to help their employees. Today we will consider:

- parental leave arrangements
- care policies
- career breaks
- other types of assistance
- flexible benefits

Parental leave arrangements

Maternity leave
Maternity leave is the longest standing of all parental leave arrangements and is the only one currently protected by law. All female employees are entitled to 14 weeks' statutory maternity leave and, if they have been with an employer for at least two years by the beginning of the 11th week before the expected week of the birth, are entitled to up to 40 weeks leave in total (from 11 weeks before the

THURSDAY

birth and up to 29 weeks afterwards). Many employers, however, offer more favourable terms (some waive the requirement to work for two years before entitlement to the extended leave is available).

Paternity leave
Although there is no legal obligation for an employer to grant paternity leave, many organisations recognise that at a time of such dramatic change in personal circumstances, a paid break can be of great help. Normally, fathers are allowed to take up to five days' paid leave within the first month of their child's life. The number of organisations offering paternity leave continues to grow.

Adoption leave
As the number of adoptions diminishes, there is much less demand for paid leave in this situation. Where formal adoption leave is available, it is often treated on the same basis as maternity or paternity leave. Organisations which have no formal policy may choose to deal with individual requests on demand.

THURSDAY

Parental leave
The European Parental Leave Directive is due to be implemented in the UK by the year 2000. It offers all parents who have been with their current employer for more than one year the right to two types of leave:

1 *parental leave* – consisting of three months' unpaid leave on the birth or adoption of a child. The time limit for taking this leave is currently a matter of discussion in the UK, but the Directive suggests it can be taken at any time up to the child's eighth birthday;
2 *leave for urgent family reasons* – employees will be entitled to take a certain amount of time in case of urgent family reasons (probably sickness or accidents). Limits to entitlement to this type of leave have yet to be decided.

Care policies

When employers and employees think of care policies, they usually think of childcare. Demographic changes, however, mean that many employees now have elder-care responsibilities in addition to, or instead of, childcare. Although there is common ground between the two issues, we will consider them independently.

Childcare
Access to affordable, good-quality childcare is a major preoccupation for many parents. This is especially true now that more than half of women with children under the age of five are in employment. Recent research carried out by the Daycare Trust has shown that over a third of women who give up their jobs after having a baby do so because adequate childcare is so expensive. Around one in ten employers currently provide staff with practical childcare

support, and a range of options exist for those organisations wishing to offer assistance:

- *information* – the service of providing information about the availability of childcare can be run by the personnel department or contracted out to a specialist organisation.
- *workplace nurseries* – usually on-site or close to the premises, these are provided by the employer. They can be run in-house or outsourced to a childcare agency. Often, such nurseries are established in partnership with another firm, which means costs are shared.
- *purchased places in local nurseries* – employers who buy places in local nurseries ensure their employees are able to find a place for their child. The costs of such a place may be absorbed by the employer or passed on to the employee.
- *childcare allowance* – an additional sum of money is paid to an employee specifically to help meet the costs of childcare. Childcare vouchers (which operate in a similar way to luncheon vouchers and are issued by the same organisation) are an alternative method of payment, and can be used for any type of childcare provision.
- *holiday and after-school provision* – as children become older, the costs of childcare decrease. Purchasing places on play-schemes, or running a scheme in-house, is something many organisations feel is a valuable way to encourage parents back to work.
- *responsibility breaks* (see the section on career breaks on pages 61–63)

Elder care

Fewer organisations offer help with elder-care responsibilities than with childcare, but with an

THURSDAY

increasingly ageing population, this is an area in which demand is sure to grow. Carers of the elderly often experience unique problems. Carer and dependant may live in different households at some distance from each other. This results in extra travelling time which may lead to added stress. The need for care may just be short-term or may continue indefinitely – which again can add to stress on the part of the carer. Many employees in this situation feel unable to talk about their caring situation with their employer, which can result in an increase in absenteeism without any overt explanation.

A variety of options exist to help carers of the elderly:

- *emergency carers leave* – this allows employees to take a period of leave (usually unpaid) to cope with a relatively short-term crisis (typically no longer than six weeks).
- *responsibility breaks* – responsibility breaks of up to two years are offered by some employers as a way in which employees who might otherwise be forced to leave work are allowed long-term unpaid leave to care for a relative. Normally there is a requirement for the employee to work for a few weeks each year in order to keep in touch with the workplace and have some respite from their caring responsibilities.
- *information services* – many people who find themselves caring for an elderly dependant are unaware of the range of services and benefits to which they may be entitled and do not know of organisations which may be able to help them. The personnel department may be able to hold a stock of information or contract out such a service.

THURSDAY

- *day care centres* - these are similar to workplace nurseries but are rarely provided by employers due to the variety of needs of the elderly. It is more usual for allowances to be paid to enable employees to find the most appropriate care for their elderly dependants.

The following checklist suggests best practice in setting up child- and elder-care policies.

1 *Examine the short- and long-term needs for the provision of care.*
2 *Ensure senior management is committed to the implementation of a policy.* For a care policy to reap business benefits, it must be a long-term commitment, and as such may not bring immediately obvious benefits. Without senior management commitment, any such policy has little chance of success.
3 *Research all the options.* All the options for a care policy must be researched. Ascertain the probable costs and any governing legislation of each, and establish which options are already provided near the workplace. Consider, too, the geographic spread of employees – would they prefer care to be provided closer to home rather than work, or vice versa?
4 *Consult with employees.* Explain the reasons behind the decision to implement such a policy, and explain the range of options.
5 *Draw up a plan for the policy.* This needs to detail the scope of provision and include timescales, costs to be borne by the organisation and those passed to employees, and details of organisations (such as

T H U R S D A Y

> Social Services) who may need to be informed about your plans.
> 6 *Launch the scheme*. Provide advance notice for registration for the scheme (as notice may need to be given to a current day-care provider). If possible, allow for some future expansion of the scheme if sufficient demand is experienced.

(Take a look at Saturday for more general information on implementation.)

Career breaks

Career breaks can be taken for a number of reasons (see Friday for details of secondments and sabbaticals). Today we consider career breaks taken to care for young children or other dependent relatives, with the intention of returning to the same employer in the future.

THURSDAY

Employers recognise that offering a career break is a method through which they can retain staff who would otherwise feel forced to leave employment. Although career breaks are usually open to all employees, they are most often taken by women. Acceptance on a career break is normally at management discretion, which means that employees in those positions requiring particular expertise or which are hard to fill are more likely to be given a break.

Career breaks of two years are the norm, although some employers allow up to five years to be taken. Only one break per employee is normally permitted. Frequently, employees taking a career break are required to resign from the organisation on the understanding that at the end of their career break a similar position will be made available to them with comparable terms and conditions. Other employers merely suspend the contract of employment for the duration. Some require the employee to work for a short period of time each year of the break. This means that the expertise of the employee remains available to the organisation, they maintain their skills, they do not lose touch with their workplace and colleagues.

Sample dependency break policy

Employees whose circumstances change because they become responsible for caring for a dependant may need leave of absence for a period of time.

A dependency break scheme is available to men and women of all categories and levels who have completed a minimum of two years' continuous service. Acceptance on the scheme will be based on performance, and at the discretion of line and personnel

THURSDAY

> management. For those accepted on the scheme, the Company will undertake to provide a position at the end of the 'Dependency Break'. Eligible employees are normally entitled to one dependency break only during their employment with the Company, irrespective of the length of break.
>
> The length of the dependency break should be discussed on an individual basis, up to a maximum of five years. The individual will resign from the Company and therefore the years on dependency break will not count as service for the calculation of benefits.
>
> Each year the individual must work a minimum number of hours equivalent to two of their original working weeks, at a mutually convenient time and pattern of hours. This work will be on a temporary employment basis. No other form of paid employment should be undertaken during the dependency break without prior consultation with the personnel manager. Contact will be maintained throughout the dependency break by the relevant store or department.

Other types of assistance

Recognising the stresses and demands placed on employees by the pace of life today, some employers have introduced other methods of helping their employees. Confidential counselling lines operated by external organisations are used by many employers, and some are enabling their employees to make use of 'concierge' services (which can deliver and pick up dry cleaning, wait at home for the plumber or collect parcels) in an effort to reduce the amount of time employees spend on time-consuming domestic activities.

THURSDAY

Flexible benefits

'Flexible' (otherwise known as 'flex' or 'cafeteria') benefit schemes were originally established during the 1980s in America. In the UK they are found across a wide range of company sizes and industry sectors, although they are most likely to be set up in large organisations. As many as 68 per cent of organisations now have some form of flexible benefit scheme.

Such arrangements allow employees to choose (within limits) the composition of their benefits package. Core benefits (such as basic pension provision and an amount of annual leave) are supplemented by a range of extra benefits, such as childcare vouchers, car breakdown cover and sports-club membership – items which very rarely feature in a traditional benefits package.

There are pros and cons in implementing such a scheme. Administering a flex package is complex and costly. Greater control of costs is possible via a flex scheme, however, and a clearer picture of the total cost and advantage of each benefit offered can be obtained. If employees choose the benefits most appropriate to their individual circumstances, better value for money is obtained by the organisation – and individuals feel that they are receiving something of relevance to them. For example, a parent may choose to take part of their benefits package in childcare vouchers, whilst a dual-income couple might rationalise their benefits (only one opting for health insurance which covers both themselves and their partner, and the other choosing car breakdown cover).

Flexible benefit schemes can also help address some of the negative feelings felt by some groups who may feel discriminated against, such as full-timers or childless people.

Summary

Today we have looked at some of the policies which organisations may introduce to help their employees balance working and caring responsibilities, including the provision of some forms of extended unpaid leave. Tomorrow we will examine other forms of extended leave – specifically secondments and sabbaticals.

FRIDAY

Secondments and sabbaticals

Today we shall focus on secondments (which are principally used as a means of career development) and on sabbaticals (which give people a break from routine to pursue professional or personal interests). We shall consider:

- secondments:
  - the benefits of secondment
  - the risks of secondment
  - managing secondments
  - exchanges and job swaps
- sabbatical leave

Secondments

A secondment is the temporary loan or attachment of an employee from one organisation to another, or to a different part of the same organisation, for a specific purpose, for a defined length of time. Once seen as a form of corporate benevolence or as a career dead-end, secondments are now increasingly recognised as an important means of employee development – for in today's flatter organisations, there are fewer opportunities for people to grow through promotion.

Traditional secondments take place on a full-time basis and last between one and three years. Shorter secondments which focus on a specific project are more common and may be staffed on a part-time basis of one day a week. The employees chosen for longer secondments tend to be high fliers or middle managers who have been with the firm for

FRIDAY

several years. Shorter secondments normally involve more junior staff. Usually, secondments entail a big organisation supporting a smaller one, perhaps a small business, a charity, or an arts organisation.

Some individuals arrange their own secondments. In this situation, the employer grants a leave of absence but usually gives no further help or support. Although these arrangements can be very successful, there are risks involved (see pages 69–71 below).

The benefits of secondment
To be a success, secondment has to benefit all parties. For the individual, secondment gives the opportunity to:

- increase confidence through learning that skills are transferable
- build upon existing skills, knowledge, interests and experience and develop new skills, such as dealing with the media

FRIDAY

- undertake a different, or higher, range of responsibilities, such as becoming involved in strategic rather than operational issues
- work in a different environment and culture, thereby developing a wider perspective and becoming more adaptable
- build up a new network of contacts
- watch, and learn from, alternative management practices and styles
- assess career prospects

For the host, secondment:

- gives access to expertise that may not otherwise be affordable
- provides extra labour (but this should be for a clearly defined purpose)
- brings in a new external perspective on the organisation (new blood, with new ideas)

For the employer, secondment:

- demonstrates a commitment to self-development
- gives individuals practical development opportunities which are otherwise unavailable
- can increase morale as staff return with an increased sense of fulfilment
- enables information about the culture, methods and knowledge of other organisations to be gathered
- raises the corporate profile by demonstrating commitment to the community
- may bring prestige if associated with high-profile organisations or causes

FRIDAY

The risks of secondment

There are also risks for the employer in a secondment project, however:

- Apart from paying the secondee's salary, there are other costs involved, such as those of filling the secondee's post while they are away.
- By its very nature, a secondment involves passing on expertise to another organisation. Secondments may not be appropriate, therefore, where sensitive or competitive information is involved.
- The host organisation is looking for someone who can make their project a success. The secondee must therefore be sufficiently self-motivated to adapt to another situation and other people quickly. If they do not do so, then the secondment fails and reflects badly on their employer.
- If new skills are not recognised, and ways are not found to use them on the secondee's return, then some potential benefits will be lost.
- The host may ask the individual to extend the duration of the secondment – a delay in the employee's return may mean that they lose touch with current developments.
- The secondee may not want to return. In such a case the organisation loses the corporate knowledge which the employee has built up, perhaps over many years, as well as the increased knowledge and skills learnt on secondment.

There are also risks to the individual, as the organisation may not be prepared for the secondee's return. This is particularly true where there is no formal secondment policy in place. Various scenarios may materialise:

FRIDAY

- The organisation will inevitably change while the secondee is away, and they may get forgotten

HAVEN'T I SEEN YOU SOMEWHERE BEFORE?

- There may be no job open for the secondee, which may lead to them being made redundant in due course; or no appropriate position, which means that they will have to twiddle their thumbs
- The secondee may need to sort out their own job for their return, which involves asking around for forthcoming opportunities while still on secondment

Case study – secondment

I had reached a break point in my career and was looking for some overseas experience. In order to obtain this I took leave of absence from my UK university post and obtained a post with a university in Hong Kong. This arrangement allows me to retain my UK post but removes the associated salary and other benefits, including superannuation, while I am away. The university in Hong Kong employs me on a contractual basis which includes a gratuity to cover pension costs. I originally applied for a two-year contract but

> was then given a further two-year term. There is no possibility of a further extension of my leave of absence and I plan to return to the UK. The fact that I am on leave of absence from my UK post is of no consequence to the university in Hong Kong and there has been no contact whatsoever between the two institutions on my account – my application to the university in Hong Kong was done independently.
>
> The risks to me of taking a secondment were negligible – only that I might have had an uncomfortable couple of years to serve if I had not liked Hong Kong. On the other hand, there have been great benefits in terms of broadening my horizons and having the opportunity to work in a well-resourced university. Contact with Hong Kong, Asian, US and Australian colleagues has been very useful to me. When I return to the UK my university will gain a more experienced member of staff with (hopefully) new ideas and greater motivation. In allowing me to take a secondment they took the risk, however, that I might not choose to return and that even if I did I might find it very difficult to settle.

Managing secondments

Not all organisations have a formal secondment system. This situation is changing, however, as the importance of a well-planned process to a successful secondment is becoming recognised. The following checklist focuses on good practice in managing a secondment.

> 1 *Link the secondment programme to overall organisational objectives and the planned development of staff.* Don't use secondment as a solution for staffing problems, for example where there is no next job available for a particular person whom the organisation doesn't want to lose. Focus

FRIDAY

on the benefits you want from a secondment, and work with the individual concerned to specify objectives.

2 *Obtain line, as well as human-resource, commitment.* Without it, managers may refuse to allow certain members of staff to take part in secondments because they regard them as too valuable to lose, even for a short period.

3 *Match the person who needs development to a suitable organisation and job* – choosing the wrong individual for the wrong job will cause problems for everyone. Projects need to be well-defined so that the host organisation has realistic expectations of what can be achieved and the secondee has a clear focus for their work. Ensure that the secondee has relevant skills to carry out a demanding project which also allows them sufficient challenge to develop.

4 *Clarify terms and conditions of employment.* State any changes in terms and conditions which will apply during the secondment. Consider if there are any implications for security of employment, and pension rights.

5 *Get agreement on the individual's level of status and responsibility in the host organisation*, whether within or outside the formal structure – otherwise it can lead to the secondee becoming involved unnecessarily in company politics.

6 *Ensure that the employee maintains contact.* Appoint a mentor to take responsibility for the secondee and to offer support and advice.

FRIDAY

Keep in touch with the secondee, and encourage their colleagues to do the same.
7 *Monitor performance and results.* The responsibility for appraisal should rest with the host organisation, but agree the means of appraisal between the three parties before the secondment starts. The employer should get reports from the host organisation, perhaps twice a year. The secondee should be encouraged to keep a log, and to take stock of their learning and development on a regular basis. The appraisal process ensures that the secondee's performance can be linked to the employer's salary review, and that the employer can keep in touch with the skills being developed, so that these can be recognised, and best use made of them, on the secondee's return.

Exchanges and job swaps

Exchanges are another form of secondment. Sometimes they take place within large multinational companies in order to spread ideas and to give individuals international experience. In other cases they are carried out on a one-to-one basis between two people in different organisations, usually as part of a desire to live and work abroad for a period. To set up such an exchange, an individual needs to gain approval for the idea and then find a good match in terms of qualifications, skills and experience. Participants and management must agree on the objectives of the exchange, its duration, and other factors such as training, pay and holiday arrangements.

FRIDAY

Case study – Skill Swap

Skill swap is a programme offering short-term secondments, run within the National Health Service. It enables trusts and health authorities to carry out clearly defined projects at a fraction of the cost of employing external consultants, while offering individuals opportunities for career development. Originally, secondments were initiated by the host organisations, but increasingly they start with individuals, often as part of an existing development programme. All parties (the host organisation, the employer and the individual) are given practical assistance by the Salomons Centre – an independent centre, offering training, education, research and consultancy, which is part of Canterbury Christ Church College. The Salomons Centre gives advice and help in setting up the project (which includes ensuring that the individual is of the right calibre and promoting them to relevant organisations), during the secondment itself and in evaluating the experience at the end.

FRIDAY

> Skill Swap is continually evolving. The Salomons Centre coordinates the lessons learnt about managing secondments and feeds this knowledge into new programmes. For example, the host organisation, rather than Skill Swap, is now required to pay employers for the cost of cover whilst the secondee is away. This encourages the perception of secondees as internal consultants, rather than as a free resource. Several organisations within the NHS are starting to apply the concepts of Skill Swap to suit the local situation. For example, the former NHS Women's Unit commissioned a programme specifically to develop female middle and senior managers.
>
> The consensus from all sides which have taken part in the 28 secondments so far has been very positive, with many of the projects continuing after the initial six months. Most secondees have not returned to their original jobs, regarding this as a positive development, but many have stayed within the NHS, ensuring that the overall skills available across a national service are increasing.
>
> *Source:* Rick Stern, Skill Swap Programme Director, Salomons Centre.
> Tel: 01892 515152

Sabbatical leave

Sabbatical leave allows extended time away from work which is in addition to the annual holiday entitlement. It may be paid or unpaid. (Where someone is not in permanent employment, they may choose to give themselves sabbatical leave by taking a break in between contracts.) Periods of sabbatical leave can range from a few weeks to a year, but typically last three months. In America, some large companies such as AT&T, McDonalds, Apple and Wells Fargo Bank have experimented with formal programmes. In the UK, ad hoc arrangements, covered by normal leave policies, are still the norm.

FRIDAY

There are various reasons why individuals take sabbatical leave. It enables some to take a rest by enjoying an extended holiday, or by travelling overseas or by pursuing a hobby. Others use the opportunity to carry out voluntary work for the community or to undertake an educational or development activity. In universities, academics use sabbaticals to carry out research, away from the pressures of teaching.

People qualify for sabbatical leave usually by length of service and are usually full-time senior or managerial staff. Common stipulations on the employer's part are that employees must have demonstrated a previous commitment to the activity they will undertake in their time away and that the activity should not be for financial profit, or adversely affect the employer.

Employers grant sabbatical leave as it helps to:

- reward long-serving employees
- keep employees who might otherwise leave – it makes people feel good about their employer
- give employees a break and a rest, so that they come back fresher and more creative, perhaps with a different perspective, also minimising sick leave
- develop employees and give them additional skills and wider experience

There are also various concerns expressed by both employers and individuals, however:

- The employer has to pay the costs of providing cover whilst the employee is away
- Colleagues may resent the absence, particularly if they have to cover

FRIDAY

- The individual may lose touch with developments at work or in their profession
- They may find it difficult to plan for a sabbatical because of pressures of work, and find it difficult to return to routine when the sabbatical comes to an end
- Sabbaticals can be seen to tackle the symptoms of stress rather than the cause

Case study – a sabbatical

I started skiing in my twenties and was immediately hooked on this brilliant and exhilarating sport. As I had only just embarked on my career, however, I resigned myself to annual holidays. A few years later a British ski instructor friend of mine suggested that I run a small chalet company in France during the following winter. The idea really appealed to me but how could I risk giving up my job with a company for whom I had worked for many years, with all the accumulated benefits? I was worried that I might find it difficult to get a job when I got back.

Then someone suggested I ask for time off as a sabbatical. OK I would ask but this doesn't happen in the UK. I thought it best to raise the subject with my director as my immediate bosses might not be in a position to agree to something which would set a precedent and because they place more importance on achieving immediate targets than on the long-term picture. I explained to my director that I had got the opportunity to realise a life-long ambition and waited for the 'No!' To my surprise and delight he was very open to the idea and, subject to certain technicalities, he agreed that I could take five months off. His worry was that there would now be a long queue of people outside his office asking for the same thing. To avoid this, he made it clear to everyone that a sabbatical was granted to me following extended service and commitment and to achieve a specific goal. He believed the company should take a

FRIDAY

forward-looking view and that offering a break provides an appropriate reward or inducement for loyalty and commitment. It might also help in retaining staff who found they could not balance career aspirations with personal ones.

Once my sabbatical was agreed, I started making plans for the winter. It turned out to be a thoroughly enjoyable season, with my meeting some lovely people and with some fabulous skiing. The sabbatical gave me an invaluable experience about managing and running a small business in a different country and about life in general.

Once I returned to work, I managed to knuckle down to it, although of course I hankered after the freedom of the Alps. The type of work we were undertaking during my first couple of months back wasn't something I particularly enjoyed, but the fact that I had had a break helped me get through the bad patch rather than making matters worse.

Summary

Today we have finished our look at a range of flexible working practices by considering employment breaks which develop and refresh long-serving employees. Tomorrow we give some general advice on the implementation of flexible working options.

S A T U R D A Y

Implementing flexible working

Having looked at various kinds of flexible working, today we will give some guidance on implementation which is applicable to all schemes. We will also review some of the steps which individuals should take if they are to counteract one of the greatest dangers of flexible working: skills obsolescence. We shall consider:

- a checklist for implementing flexible working
- writing a flexible working policy
- self-development

A checklist for implementing flexible working

1 *Assess the business case.* Organisational systems and structures, including flexible working, must ultimately work to the benefit of the customer – they should augment, not obstruct, customer service. You need to judge the likely impact of flexible working on the requirements and preferences of customers. This can be assessed through:
    - direct consultation with actual and potential customers (but don't rely on what may be a partial snapshot of some users' experiences and preferences)
    - charting peaks and troughs in demand – when do the users want the service or product?
    - evaluating the type of communication needed with customers and within the business – face-to-

SATURDAY

face; by telephone; through paper memos and reports; by e-mail; or via intranets or the Internet.
- piloting arrangements (see point 11 below).

2 *Examine the corporate culture.* Many organisations still believe that the amount of time spent at the office is an indicator of commitment, productivity and results. Such organisations therefore tend to place value on time spent at work rather than on effectiveness, an approach which can undermine business goals.

Flexible workers may be seen as inefficient, uncommitted and unreliable (and enjoying better lifestyles into the bargain!). Some organisations need to change their culture to ensure that flexible working is seen as a more efficient way of working and as an opportunity to make the business more responsive to markets and customers.

SATURDAY

3. *Secure the commitment of top management.* Culture change is a gradual process. Ideally it should start with senior management setting a new vision and reinforcing it with new behaviour. This should then lead to everyone examining their own assumptions and exploring their work processes. Senior managers can assist the process by calling meetings at sensible times and leaving the office promptly rather than reinforcing a culture of 'presenteeism'.
4. *Set up a working party* to investigate and phase in changes to working practices. As part of this process, find out what other organisations have done and learn from them – don't reinvent the wheel. Nominate a co-ordinator, who can retain a general overview of the flexible working policy once it is implemented, and manage the monitoring and review procedure. Seek representatives from all levels and departments, including support sections.
5. *Draw up a profile of your existing workforce and their current hours.* This will demonstrate how much informal flexible working is already sanctioned by line managers.
6. *Consult staff and the unions.* Opinion can be sought through questionnaire surveys or working parties, but remember that people may feel more willing to air their views if senior managers are not present at exploratory meetings. If it is impractical to seek the views of all employees, make sure at least that they are all represented. Decide if you wish to seek their views on any changes they would like to see or only

SATURDAY

on certain options. Ask them to consider what effect they think flexible working will have on the business – they are probably best placed to judge the impact of introducing changes. Address concerns over whether flexible working will be imposed or voluntary, whether it will benefit or compromise employees' job security and terms of employment, and whether certain types of flexible working will contravene health and safety and other employment regulations.

7 *Be prepared for resistance to change.* Managers may dislike setting precedents and think that flexible schedules will involve more work for them. It may take time for staff to understand flexible working and to come to terms with it. It is crucial, therefore, to dispel any myths and anxieties which people have about flexible working, especially the upheaval of change itself. Overcome points of resistance by stressing benefits, but don't deny the downside. Provide role models to show how flexible working can work successfully. It is important to win the co-operation of managers because continuing management control and co-ordination is vital, so ask those in favour of flexible working to talk things over with those who are doubtful.

8 *Consider the costs.* Look at any additional costs which will be incurred, such as those of buying new equipment, as well as increased management time. Assess them in the context of business benefits, however: what would it cost you *not* to use flexibility?

9 *Design the programme* (see the following section on writing a flexible working policy).

SATURDAY

10 *Communicate the policy to all staff.* Publicise the scheme, and the reasons for introducing it, to flexible and non-flexible workers alike. Suitable media include: the corporate intranet, leaflets and posters, memos, newsletters or newspapers, job adverts and company videos.

11 *Run a pilot.* Once flexible working is adopted, it is difficult to reverse the process. To test the scheme before making it more widely available, introduce policies gradually, in selected parts of the organisation. This enables you to see if expected benefits arise and if the scheme is workable. Also, staff are more likely to accept a flexible arrangement if they know it is a time-limited experiment with a possible return to the status quo at the end, and if their experience is to be a key factor in evaluating the initiative.

> 12 *Set up a system to monitor and evaluate the scheme.* Ensure that evaluation is carried out against the business benefits sought. In order to measure success and failure, you need to assess commitment to the scheme, and its impact so far. Establish what you need to know and how you are going to obtain the information. You might ask questions such as:
> - what is the impact on customer service?
> - how has staff productivity been affected?
> - can flexible working be used more widely?
> - how can it be improved?
> - what mistakes have we made?
> - what lessons have we learned?
>
> The annual planning process is an ideal time for reviewing the organisation's overall flexibility.

Writing a flexible working policy

The policy should take the form of guidelines which ensure consistency across the organisation but allow line managers discretion in applying them. Policy guidelines should address the following issues:

1 *the scope of the policy.* Consider how flexible the organisation can afford to be, bearing in mind that the impact on the customer must be either positive or, at worst, neutral. (Don't let any slight inconveniences or small costs be seen as barriers to the adoption of flexible working practices, however.)
   - Are you willing to consider all the options for flexibility, or do you have something specific in mind?

- Will flexible working apply across the whole organisation? If not, and legal considerations apart, you will need to take care that the policy does not appear discriminatory; would staff working in one section feel jealous of the flexibility given to colleagues in another? Would childless employees feel resentful of flexibility given to parents?
- Will there be a qualifying period or age restrictions? If so, consult staff, and be open and honest about terms and conditions of eligibility for each flexible work option.

2 *changing needs*. Bear in mind that individual situations will probably change over time. For example, a mobile worker may weary of travelling and want to come back to the office; a full-time worker may need to work part-time for a period to look after a dependant.

SATURDAY

3. *workloads and timetables*. This means tackling questions such as:
   - what system will there be for arranging cover? Will you need to employ more people? Changing hours will be discredited if an individual has the same workload, if other members of the team have to pick up what is left or if the business suffers.
   - will a teleworker have to take on additional responsibilities that would have previously been carried out by support staff in the office?
   - will a mobile worker be able to visit more clients if he or she is not regularly required to come in to the office?
4. *communication channels*. Good communication is the key component of all flexible working systems. It is essential to:
   - be able to contact remote workers as fast as you can contact full-time, on-site staff, and for them to be able to respond in the same way. Communication should be supported by a proper reporting system between flexible workers and their manager and other colleagues.
   - keep in touch with employees who are away from the company for long periods of time – for example, on secondment or career breaks.
   - inform the customer of revised working arrangements, the benefits these will bring (such as increased opening hours) and limitations (such as particular individuals not always being immediately available).

SATURDAY

5. *the development of flexible workers.* Decide how you will ensure equal access to training and promotion opportunities. Monitor the career development of flexible and non-flexible workers alike by encouraging them to define their own work/career expectations and supporting them in developing the skills and attributes which will enhance their employability inside and outside the organisation. Make sure that the timing and methods of training offered are suitable for flexible workers. Appraisal systems may need to be adapted – for example, individuals carrying out a job share must be appraised on how effectively the arrangement is working, as well as being appraised on their own performance. Greater emphasis should be placed on work outputs, such as customer service, rather than on work inputs, such as time.
6. *pay and benefits.* Consider how to reward flexible workers. Will the organisation, for example:
    - replace hourly rates with annual salaries in an annual-hours system?
    - pay teleworkers on the number of hours worked or on productivity?
    - grant paid or non-paid leave for sabbaticals?
7. *contracts of employment.* Revise contracts of employment where necessary, checking that they are fair and lawful to avoid unfair dismissal and other employment claims. It is essential to keep up-to-date with legislation.
8. *recruitment.* Question traditional practices such as replacing a full-time employee with another full-time employee, and consider if you could offer a flexible contract. If so, in addition to revising the job specification, you may need to tailor:

- methods of advertising
- the advert itself
- the application form
- selection procedures

Case study – implementing flexible working

During 1997 DuPont employees in Europe were introduced to a comprehensive work/life programme tailored to meet their personal and working requirements. The two key areas covered in the programme are flexible working and dependant care.

To demonstrate commitment to enabling employees to balance home and work lives, flexible working may be requested for a variety of reasons apart from family ones. Rozemarijn Lauressyens, who heads the work/life initiative for DuPont Europe, says 'we have been careful to develop an equable system that is not judgmental on what constitutes a deserving or less deserving request'. It is important to note that employees requesting a flexible working option need not divulge the reason for the request.

DuPont believes that the following flexible work principles are the most important.

- Flexible work practices must be designed and implemented so that they make sense for each individual function/business and accommodate individual employee and team needs. Examples are flexitime, part-time, job sharing, flexiplace, a compressed working week, and voluntary reduced hours.
- The commitment to high standards of health and safety, ethics and legal requirements must be maintained.
- Flexible work options can be requested by all employees to help them to better integrate their professional responsibilities and personal needs.

- All requests for flexible working must be given due consideration and should not be rejected without a full review process by Human Resources.
- Flexible working should not affect consideration for development opportunities.

Implementation was critical to the success of the programme and DuPont's implementation plan included the following points.

- Training and familiarisation meetings for DuPont Human Resource supervisors in Europe.
- These supervisors should act as work/life administrators for all Strategic Business Units and functions.
- Training and familiarisation for supervisors and employees at the different sites so that everyone knows exactly what is available at their particular location.
- Communication through the DuPont European Communication Network.

Source: Geraldine Bown, Managing Director, The Domino Consultancy Limited, Tel: 01509 650505. Ms Bown is working with DuPont Europe on their Diversity, Harassment and Work/Life initiatives.

Self-development

As organisations change, so must employees. According to William Bridges, 'workers must begin to think of themselves as independent contractors, not lifetime employees. True security comes not from clinging to a job, but from doing the work you are best at for the employers who need it.' (*The Times*, 16 October 1997.)

SATURDAY

The broader the range of skills you have, the better your own future prospects and those of the business for which you work. Assess the shelf-life of your skills – how long will it be before a new technology creates the need for new skills and renders the old ones obsolete? The following recommendations for individuals come from recent research published by the Institute of Management which has looked at the changing nature of the relationship between employee and organisation.

- *Change*: you must be prepared for change and be willing to embrace it.
- *Continuing professional development:* aim to continually develop your competencies (which should include a range of transferable skills such as computer literacy, information management, interpersonal skills, communication techniques, languages, teamworking, negotiation, financial management and strategic analysis). This may well involve a personal investment of time, energy and money.

SATURDAY

- *Networking:* professional networks, both formal and informal, can help keep you up-to-date and familiar with current issues and thinking while enhancing your career-development prospects.
- *Time management:* effective time management enables you to improve your efficiency, thus maximising your worth to the organisation and time for life outside work.

Remember that flexibility can open up new prospects, but ultimately the real key to success lies in your attitude towards your own development.

Summary

Flexible working is not an easy option for responsible organisations. It requires enhanced skills, particularly in the management of change, communication and team-building. The reward is that its successful implementation can become a form of competitive advantage, in terms of improving productivity and customer service, as well as in achieving a committed workforce. For individuals, it brings the power to organise both their work and personal lives in a more efficient and resourceful way appropriate to their situation.

Further *Successful Business in a Week* **titles all at £6.99.** A complete listing of all titles can be obtained from Katie Ingram on 0171 873 6261.

ISBN	Title		ISBN	Title	
0 340 71205 8	Appraisals in a Week	❏	0 340 67922 0	Planning for Retirement in a Week	❏
0 340 70546 9	Assertiveness in a Week	❏	0 340 70541 8	Planning Your Own Career in a Week	❏
0 340 72077 8	Business Growth in a Week	❏			
0 340 71199 X	Business Plans in a Week	❏	0 340 70544 2	Presentation in a Week	❏
0 340 59813 1	Business Writing in a Week	❏	0 340 65563 1	Process Management in a Week	❏
0 340 71200 7	Communication at Work in a Week	❏	0 340 70539 6	Project Management in a Week	❏
0 340 71196 5	Customer Care in a Week	❏	0 340 64761 2	Problem Solving in a Week	❏
0 340 70543 4	CVs in a Week	❏	0 340 56479 2	Public Relations in a Week	❏
0 340 72076 X	Dealing with Difficult People in a Week		0 340 62738 7	Purchasing in a Week	❏
			0 340 71198 1	Report Writing in a Week	❏
0 340 63154 6	Decision Making in a Week	❏	0 340 70538 8	Selling in a Week	❏
0 340 64330 7	Empowerment in a Week	❏	0 340 67397 4	Selling on the Internet in a Week	❏
0 340 71192 2	Finance for Non-Financial Managers in a Week	❏	0 340 71201 5	Stress Management in a Week	❏
			0 340 70542 6	Succeeding at Interviews in a Week	❏
0 340 71189 2	Flexible Working in a Week	❏	0 340 64342 0	Teambuilding in a Week	❏
0 340 67925 5	Fundraising and Sponsorship in a Week	❏	0 340 70547 7	Time Management in a Week	❏
			0 340 71195 7	Training in a Week	❏
0 340 71204 X	Going Freelance in a Week	❏	0 340 71197 3	Understanding Benchmarking in a Week	❏
0 340 65487 2	Human Resource Management in a Week	❏			
			0 340 70540 X	Understanding Business on the Internet in a Week	❏
0 340 59812 3	Interviewing in a Week	❏			
0 340 71179 5	Intranets in a Week	❏	0 340 62103 6	Understanding Business Process Re-engineering in a Week	❏
0 340 63152 X	Introducing Management in a Week	❏			
0 340 62742 5	Introduction to Bookkeeping and Accounting in a Week	❏	0 340 71173 6	Understanding Management Gurus in a Week	❏
0 340 60895 1	Leadership in a Week	❏	0 340 71174 4	Understanding Mind Maps® in a Week	❏
0 340 65503 8	Managing Change in a Week	❏			
0 340 70537 X	Marketing in a Week	❏	0 340 71123 X	Understanding Neuro-Linguistic Programming in a Week	❏
0 340 67924 7	Marketing Plans in a Week	❏			
0 340 57466 6	Market Research in a Week	❏	0 340 65504 6	Understanding Statistics in a Week	❏
0 340 60894 3	Meetings in a Week	❏	0 340 71191 4	Understanding Total Quality Management in a Week	❏
0 340 61137 5	Mentoring in a Week	❏			
0 340 57522 0	Motivation in a Week	❏	0 340 62102 8	Understanding VAT in a Week	❏
0 340 70545 0	Negotiating in a Week	❏	0 340 70508 6	Web Sites in a Week	❏
0 340 64341 2	Networking in a Week	❏			

All Hodder & Stoughton books are available from your local bookshop or can be ordered direct from the publisher. Just tick the titles you want and fill in the form below. Prices and availability subject to change without notice.

To: Hodder & Stoughton Ltd, Cash Sales Department, Bookpoint, 39 Milton Park, Abingdon, Oxon, OX14 4TD. If you have a credit card you may order by telephone – 01235 400414.

E-mail address: orders@bookpoint.co.uk

Please enclose a cheque or postal order made payable to Bookpoint Ltd to the value of the cover price and allow the following for postage and packaging:

UK & BFPO: £1.00 for the first book, 50p for the second book and 30p for each additional book ordered up to a maximum charge of £3.00.

OVERSEAS & EIRE: £2.00 for the first book, £1.00 for the second book and 50p for each additional book.

Name: ....

Address: ....

....

If you would prefer to pay by credit card, please complete:

Please debit my Visa/Mastercard/Diner's Card/American Express (delete as appropriate) card no:

☐☐☐☐☐☐☐☐☐☐☐☐☐☐☐☐

Signature .... Expiry Date ....